MW01491475

Language & Cognition Resources, LLC
378 Squire Lane,
Lititz, PA 17543
www.TotalParticipationTechniques.com
info@totalparticipationtechniques.com

Cover Design by Alyssa Dill and Nancy Mata

Page Layout by Alyssa Dill and Nancy Mata

Publishing Consultant & Graphic Designer, Nancy Mata (*nancy.mata@ millersville.edu*)

Printed in the United States of America

ISBN: 978-0-9971563-0-0

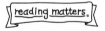

Additional copies of this text can be ordered through
www.readingmatters.net or by calling toll free 1-888-255-6665.

Language & Cognition Resources
Lititz, PA
www.TotalParticipationTechniques.com

We've worked with some amazing principals and district leaders over the years. We'd like to dedicate this book to you, principals who take advantage of every opportunity to sharpen your skills as instructional leaders.

Praise for Four Things Every Principal Should Know About English Language Learners

"This resource is a perfect, quick and easy desk reference for all principals (and central administrators). The tools shared in this book are ideal for team meetings, so that the focus remains on what ELLs need… Several years ago, I was introduced to the C.H.A.T.S. Framework during a summer symposium. Since that time, I have been a 'disciple' of sorts of the perspective, since it truly made all the difference in the instructional leadership I offered my staff…With the publication of this book, I am once again inspired!"

Dr. Nancy A. Aronson
Retired Elementary Principal
Education Consultant

"While the book is geared toward school principals, I found the content very applicable in my role as district administrator. The tips and strategies presented in the book can be scaled to any size school or district."

Brett F. Stark
Director of Curriculum
Frederick County Public Schools, MD

"A few of my favorite features of the text are its ease of readability, the way crucial background information is embedded within the strategies offered, and the fact that the Himmeles provide solutions to present-day challenges of working with ELLs."

Doreen Milot
Supervisor of ESL and District Support Consultant
Schuylkill Intermediate Unit, PA

"As a faculty member preparing future principals, I look forward to utilizing the book *Four Things Every Principal Should Know about English Language Learners* by Drs. Persida & William Himmele. Many of my students teach in districts where there are limited opportunities to interact with ELL students, and this exposure for them is vital as future school leaders."

Dr. Tiffany Wright
Co-Director, Doctorate in Educational Leadership
Millersville University, PA

"The background information and instructional strategies provided to meet the needs of our ELL students was not within the coursework for becoming a principal. After reading *Four Things Every Principal Should Know About English Language Learners*, I feel that I am in a much better position to guide my staff."

Dr. Kimberly Stoltz
Principal – Yorkshire Elementary
York Suburban School District, PA

"As a former principal who has led in times of high accountability... I loved the simplicity of this read. With 4 easy think-abouts guiding the work, the organization of the content was supported by the 'in a nutshell' summaries. I also loved the key questions for principal leaders and the other organizers and resources within each section. This is truly a great 'getting started' book that provides key take-aways that a principal could use immediately."

Jamie Aliveto
Director, System Accountability and School Improvement
Frederick County Public Schools, MD

"As a public educator and advocate for English language learners, this book is a must read. Himmele and Himmele provide a comprehensive, practical, and easy to read reference for directly and positively impacting classroom environments and student achievement."

Dr. Anita de la Isla
Professional Development Coordinator
Irving Indpendent School District, TX

Four Things Every Principal Should Know About English Language Learners

An easy-read for busy administrators

Pérsida Himmele, Ph.D. &
William Himmele, Ph.D.

with a forward by Thomas R. Hoerr, Ph.D.

Table of contents

Forward

Throughout this book, Pérsida and Bill Himmele provide a great service to principals of schools with students for whom English is not a native language. The authors appreciate the power of principals and the role of strong leadership, and they also understand that, in order to be truly effective, a principal works with her faculty. Leadership, whether associated with ELLs or not, is built upon listening and caring, and that idea comes through very strongly.

The Himmeles remind us that the skills and backgrounds of our students must be considered in planning instruction. While this may seem obvious, too often it does not happen. That's not from any malice; rather, the pace of the day results in principals and teachers only sharing snippets of experiences, as if we were passing ships on the sea. The differences in the kinds of skills possessed by ELL students are well delineated, beginning with survival English, and these skill levels frame how programs should be developed and instruction delivered. The authors remind us that in determining how ELL students are to be grouped, we need to ask our teachers, "What do the students need?" and then to be sure to listen to their responses. The answers will inform caseload, groupings, and the kinds of services that are offered.

Sometimes the simplest steps are the hardest!

The authors advocate principals observing ELL classes – irrespective of the principal's own proficiencies in other languages or background in ELL. Wisely, they understand that a principal can help teachers by providing feedback on how the classroom is structured and how students are responding to instruction. Sometimes teachers can be too immersed in their instruction or classroom organization to be able to objectively evaluate it, but it can be relatively easy for a visitor to see what is working and what might be improved. (This is true for all teachers in all classrooms, but I expect it may be even more the case in an ELL situation because there is an additional barrier between the teacher and learner.) The questions provided by the Himmeles will be very helpful to principals.

I appreciated the distinction made between conversational and academic language. Of course, we hope that our students will succeed and we tend to seek signs of progress; thus we can confuse conversational comfort with academic proficiency.

Their statement that educators may "believe that because Marcos and Peter sound the same, their performances should also be the same" is fraught with implications for our expectations of students and supervision of teachers.

The Himmeles' CHATS framework (Content Reading Supports, Higher-Order Thinking Opportunities, Assessment, Total Participation, and Scaffolds) is a wonderful tool for remembering the various ways that instruction can be framed and students supported. Their statement, "Metacognitive skills are critical, because the students have to be just as proactive about their learning as their teachers are, and just as intentional about building their own academic language as are their teachers" is a wonderful compass.

This book is rich with ideas, insights, and strategies. Thanks to the Himmeles for their ideas and energy!

Thomas R. Hoerr, Ph.D
Emeritus Head of the New City School
Author of *Becoming a Multiple Intelligences School*, *The Art of School Leadership*, *School Leadership for the Future*, *Fostering Grit*, and "The Principal Connection" column in *Educational Leadership*

Acknowledgements

We are so blessed to have wonderful educators in our lives who serve as mentors, cheerleaders, and friends. This project was one that we felt passionate about, but we feared that we might be in a small minority of educators who truly cared about this topic. When we approached friends about the book, they enthusiastically offered of their time to read through the text and offer valuable feedback and suggestions. We are truly indebted to them for the way that they graciously offered to help us out.

As you read through this book, one of the things that you might notice is the ease with which the layout, the text size, and the graphics all contribute to a reader's ability to digest and recall the contents in a way that supports the text's comprehensibility and its successful impact on educational settings. A great deal of work went into making that happen, and it is all in thanks to two very special people. We'd like to thank **Nancy Mata**, Associate Professor of Graphic & Interactive Design, and her student, *Alyssa Dill*, a Millersville University Interactive & Graphic Design major, who worked diligently to produce a sharp and highly readable text that we feel is visually impressive.

Heartfelt thanks go to the following reviewers:

Dr Thomas R. Hoerr, ASCD author, school leadership expert, and "The Principal Connection" columnist for Educational Leadership. We approached Dr. Hoerr about reviewing our text, fully expecting him to turn us down. After all, we'd only met him once, and we had contacted him close to Christmas and on a tight schedule. Much to our surprise, he replied almost immediately and graciously offered to read the text and provide feedback. So, our conclusion is this: Dr. Hoerr is not only a brilliant leader, but he's also a really nice guy!

Andrea Adams, who edited both of the companion texts. Andrea started out as our children's middle school teacher and quickly became a friend for whom we have the deepest respect.

Dr. Nancy Aronson, a former elementary school principal and education consultant with whom we've worked in a collaborative relationship for several years now, and whose love and enthusiasm for learning is contagious.

Rose Cappelli, co-author of the Mentor Text book series, published by Stenhouse. Before we even met Rose, we loved her voice and her brilliant approach to guiding students in the love of words through her amazing books about writing.

Dr. Tiffany Wright, a wonderful colleague who supported us through reading and reviewing this text during a very busy time in her semester, and who pointed us in the direction of doctoral candidates who would read it and provide helpful feedback.

Brett Stark, a doctoral candidate whose experience in the midst of his county's explosive ELL growth (900% in the last decade) put him in a perfect position to review this book and offer feedback from a practical perspective.

Jamie Aliveto, a doctoral candidate with a plethora of leadership experiences. Her expertise in special education, leading as a school principal, and leading in system accountability, put her in an excellent position to provide helpful feedback.

Dr. Kimberly Stoltz, a school principal, instructional leader, and lover of books. Her enthusiasm for reading and learning are truly commendable, and we so appreciate her taking the time to read both of our companion texts.

Doreen Milot, Schuylkill county ESL supervisor, who started out as a colleague and has become our dear friend. We love her honesty and her matter-of-fact nature, which proved to be very helpful in reviewing our book!

Dr. Anita de la Isla, a professional development coordinator out of Texas. She's a lover of learning, bilingualism, and best of all …shoes! We are so appreciative of her passion for supporting ELLs through best practices and bilingual programming.

We also want to thank our wonderful children, Gabriela and Caleb, who patiently put up with our edutalk. We are so proud of how you've both turned out! We want to thank our mothers, whom we love and appreciate a little more every day. We want to thank our siblings, who truly make life's hardships so much more bearable. We love you.

Finally, we are people of faith, and we know that all of the opportunities we've had in our lives, in our vocations, and in publishing, have been gifts from God. We thank Him for what has been, we thank Him for what is, and we thank Him for what is to come.

Introduction

We want to applaud you in advance for reading this book! Seriously. We are so grateful for school leaders like you who are willing to invest your time in understanding how to support English language learners. We're especially appreciative because the students who need the most help in your school are about to get it. We're offering more than just a couple of fun activities to do with your English language learners (ELLs) — we're about to present you with four important principles that will result in better outcomes for your ELLs. We hope that these four principles will help to shape how you guide and support your students, teachers, and your programs, with the overall result of improved services and a more collective buy-in for the sake of your ELLs.

In this text, we've targeted principals and school leaders, because we know that principals and school leaders play a critical role in the success of well-run programs. Alongside this text, we've also written a companion text, *Four Things Every Teacher Should Know about English Language Learners*. The content of that text complements this one and can support you in securing a school-wide effort toward bridging the achievement gap for your ELLs. We've kept this book brief, because we know that your time is limited. Our goal was to boil down a few of the most essential components as they relate to understanding the needs of ELLs, while also providing you with references for where to get more information on topics that you feel would benefit from further elaboration. In keeping with the spirit of urgency with which this book is written, here are four things that every principal should know about ELLs.

1

The first thing you should know about ELLs

The Quality of Your Program is Highly Dependent Upon Your Expertise

Our purpose for writing this book is based on what we've seen as a pressing need to reach the stakeholders who have the potential to make the greatest difference in the quality of learning offered to English language learners. Since 2001, we have worked with several schools, counties, districts, and state departments of education, providing support with issues related to improving quality and compliance of services offered to *English language learners (ELLs)*. Over the years, we have come to realize that, when it comes to serving ELLs, teacher expertise is essential, but even teachers with the best knowledge and teaching skills are hampered by a program that is badly put together. We've also come to realize that principals are generally the people who are in the most influential position for causing change, but they often aren't equipped with the know-how to address the change that needs to happen. In the vast majority of districts with which we've worked, across various states, schools functioned as individual decision makers on how services to ELLs were provided. There existed very little consistency from school to school, and services were often provided as an afterthought, once all other services were scheduled. That's a problem, but it's a fixable problem. You, the school leader, are in a position to provide much needed clarity to the program and to ask the right questions regarding why you're doing what you're doing, and whether or not the structure of services needs to be revisited.

In terms of a school-wide effort toward ELL growth, it's important that teachers and leaders alike have an understanding of research and best practices surrounding what works with English language learners. We'll revisit what teaching that supports ELLs looks like in Chapters 3 and 4. For now, we'd like to stress the importance of your knowing what works with English language learners.

Next, what is the status of your ESL/ EAL program?

Even the very best teachers will struggle in programs that are not well constructed or that are not well supported. As we briefly discuss ELL programming, we want to first address one of the most popular questions we get: What is the difference between ESL and ELL? The quickest response to that question is that ESL typically refers to the English as a second language program, while ELL refers to the English language learner (the actual student). And, since nothing is as simple as it seems, allow us to briefly address the alphabet soup of related acronyms. States, counties, and districts vary in the acronyms used to describe the services they provide their English language learners. These are just a few of the acronyms that are popular for referring to programming: ESL (English as a second language), ESOL (English to speakers of other languages), and EAL (English as an additional language). ESL is probably the most well-known acronym. We were introduced to the acronym, EAL (English as an additional language), in Manitoba Canada. It's our favorite, because the word "additional" presents English as a bonus for a person who already has one or more languages. Because of its popularity, we'll be using ESL, but we'll also be linking it to our preferred EAL acronym, using ESL/EAL throughout this text.

Before you change anything about your offerings, talk to the teachers who are charged with providing services to your ELLs. Sometimes teachers don't know why a program isn't working; they just know that it's not working. Talking about it can provide clarity. At other points, teachers will readily provide the reasons that programs aren't working, and they'll readily provide solutions that may actually be simple for you to enact, because of your leadership role, but impossible for them to enact, since they are not in positions to affect things like schedule changes and other simple fixes. Other solutions may be more complicated. You can't expect to provide quality services if your teachers' caseloads are impossibly large. Providing quality services does take an investment in resources, which can be more complicated to change than simple schedule changes. Either way, it's important for you to know what is and is not working (for more information about grouping and caseloads, see Chapter 2). Yet, other times, the programs are working well. If they are, it's good for you to know that they are working well, and why they are working well.

Before you change anything about your offerings, talk to the teachers who are charged with providing services to your ELLs.

Ask your ESL/EAL teachers these questions:

1. With regard to the services we are offering ELLs, how are we doing?

2. Could we be doing better? If so, how?

In a nutshell...

As a school leader, you play a key role, in the quality of services that your ELLs will receive. In order to get the lay of the land, it's important that you become aware of the status of the services that your school is providing your ELLs. It's not hard to do; it often just takes the initiative to ask questions. We'll provide a more in-depth tool to do this in Chapter 2. Next, it's also important that you know what it looks like to provide quality instruction that supports ELLs in their language growth and academic learning. We'll present these topics in Chapters 3 and 4.

The second thing you should know about ELLs

ELLs Are Not All the Same, So it Matters How You Group Them

When we visit schools that practice a "pull-out" model of offering services to English language learners, one of the most perplexing and easily fixed problem-spots that we come across is that of ELLs being placed together in a group based solely on their ELL status. In other words, it is not uncommon for us to find that regardless of the students' levels of English proficiencies, they are all placed in the same ESL/ EAL pull-out group, oftentimes based on students' grade levels. Though this grouping might seem to make sense at first glance, the needs of students at various proficiency levels vary dramatically. In fact, when it comes to English language learners, the need for differentiated teaching is oftentimes greater than what you would find in a typical classroom.

A student who is newly arrived will likely need immediate support in survival English. Though the issue regarding the benefits of pull-out instruction is controversial, Krashen's review of the literature found that, when it comes to learning English, "language classes help when they are the primary source of comprehensible input. This is especially true for beginners, who often find 'real world' input too complex to understand" (Krashen, 1985, p. 13). The demands for teacher-created materials and hands-on manipulatives-based lessons are greatest for newly arrived students.

When it comes to English language learners, the need for differentiated teaching is oftentimes greater than what you would find in a typical classroom.

Because the type of instruction that your newly arrived students need is often not the same type of instruction that would benefit all learners, your newly arrived students are oftentimes the ones who benefit the most from comprehensible language instruction in an isolated setting. In contrast, an ELL who has been in English speaking schools for five years, might be struggling most with the academic language in texts, and the analysis of complex texts. As students become conversational, the classroom becomes a perfect place to develop language and content at the same time. Co-teaching environments provide opportunities for teachers to monitor content understanding for ELLs, while being able to address misunderstandings as they occur, by simply pulling a small group to the side.

Prior schooling experiences

The needs of ELLs also vary according to the prior

schooling experiences that each student brings from his or her home country. Some have learned English in their home country, but because they learned it from a Mandarin speaker, for example, who taught English using almost entirely Mandarin, their comfort with seeing English in print is greater than hearing it in its spoken form. Yet other ELLs bring a strong academic foundation in their home language, where academic concepts are currently undergoing a process of re-labeling. These students might actually surprise you with big words thrown into sentences that are grammatically inaccurate. For example, "The man sit in automobile." Monitoring the varying needs of English language learners relies on teacher expertise, consistent checks for understanding, and placement of ELLs in environments that best support their content and language needs. In essence, this shifts the view from that of specific isolated classrooms being identified as ESL/EAL classrooms, to every single classroom being able to support the needs of English language learners. To understand the varying needs of ELLs, Freeman, Freeman, and Mercuri (2002) describe three types of English learners according to the students' prior schooling experiences. They are described in **Figure 2.1**.

What do they need?

All that being said, learning a language is incredibly complex. Grouping students based solely on their ELL label is counterproductive. To expect an ESL/EAL pull out lesson to meet the needs of the various ELL types who are at differing proficiency levels is placing unrealistic demands on ESL/EAL teachers, and it wastes some students' time with skills that are much too easy, while wasting other students' time with skills that they are not ready to acquire. We have often said, "One of the biggest mistakes that teachers make, is that they teach a great lesson to the wrong students." The question, "What do they need?" ought to drive your grouping decisions. In other words, when it comes to providing supplemental support outside of the classroom (pull-out services) students should be placed with somewhat similar age groups, but grade level should not be the deciding factor in how you group your students. For many students, what they need just happens to be scaffolded content instruction that is delivered right alongside their non-ELL peers. This is increasingly true as ELLs progress in their acquisition of English conversational skills.

The question, "What do they need?" ought to drive your grouping decisions.

In **Figure 2.2**, we provide a simple table that is meant to help you, together with your ESL/EAL teachers, to make grouping decisions based on somewhat similar ages and somewhat similar needs. For each box, write the names of the ELL students. For schools with high numbers of ELLs, simply write the number of students. Then collaboratively, alongside your ESL/EAL teachers, divide the students into groups based on similar needs. Your ESL/EAL teachers will still need to differentiate, based on the 4 language domains that will be the lessons' foci (listening, speaking, reading and writing), but the differentiation will be doable as compared to grouping students together as one large group, or grouping them by age rather than needs. Once you've gone through the task of regrouping students on paper, be ready to be flexible, because

Figure 2.1

Three Types of English Language Learners
adapted from Freeman, Freeman, & Mercuri, 2002

Type of ELL	Brief description
Newly arrived with adequate schooling	Students who have adequate schooling in their home languages have often acquired age-appropriate academic language in their home languages. This provides a tremendous advantage, since they are able to transfer much of their learning into a second language. Their ability to "crack the code" of literacy in English is facilitated by having already "cracked the code" of literacy in their home languages. This is true even when the languages are significantly dissimilar (Himmele & Himmele, 2009).
Newly arrived with limited formal schooling	Typically, students who arrive with limited or interrupted schooling have acquired conversational proficiency in their home languages, but lack academic proficiency. They have academic gaps present in their home languages that negatively affect their ability to transfer literacy skills and content-related concepts.
Long-term English learner	Long-term English learners have been in the U.S. for seven or more years. They have conversational proficiency in both English and their home languages, but they lack academic proficiency in both languages. With 65% of English language learners being born in the U.S. (Swanson, 2009), long-term English learners make up the majority of ELLs in U.S. schools.

Major academic challenges

Students with adequate schooling in their home languages go through a process of relabeling and drawing upon academic skills that worked for them when learning in their home languages. The transition to a new language and vastly different culture may be inherently stressful, for obvious reasons, but they've tasted academic success in their home languages, and they are able to transfer their concept knowledge and academic language into English. They face the fewest academic challenges when compared to their ELL peers.

Imagine the hurdles faced by a sixth grade ELL entering school for the very first time. Students with limited formal schooling are oftentimes quick to be referred for learning disabilities, when in reality, the challenges that they face are due to lack of academic exposure. They face the greatest challenges of all their ELL peers, and becoming literate in English is an exceedingly difficult task because they have not yet mastered literacy in their home languages.

Because they lack academic proficiency in their home languages, long-term English learners struggle with acquiring academic proficiency in English. They struggle in reading and literacy-dependent work. While they may be successful in the primary grades, as content becomes more dependent on academic reading and writing, their success declines. Long-term English learners benefit from the types of teaching practices that will be introduced in Chapter 4 of this text.

Figure 2.2   Creating needs-based student groups

Student groupings by proficiency & approximate age

Grade level	Starting	Emerging	
Each grade level gets one row			

Developing	Expanding	Bridging

the groups will need to change as the students' needs change. Remember that the question, "What do they need?" ought to drive your grouping decisions.

Taking the temperature of your ESL/EAL program

The most important thing that we believe principals need to do, to ensure quality programs, is to understand how the program is put together: Who is being served? How often are they being served? How are they being served?

The simplest way to measure this is to ask the teachers who actually provide the services. In **Figure 2.3**, we've included a simple tool that has allowed us to quickly understand programs and how they are designed.

How many hours?

As you review this information, you'll undoubtedly be asking yourself, how much ESL/EAL instruction should your ELLs be getting? The answer is actually a little more complicated than it may at first appear. In some cases, where content is being delivered by ESL certified teachers in content classrooms, the time in those classes will count toward the students ESL/EAL recommended hours. Your state will likely have a statement with the recommended hours of instruction for English language learners. For example, some northeastern states have recommendations that range from two to three hours for new arrivals to one hour for students with more advanced language proficiencies. For example, in Rhode Island, newcomers and beginners should receive a minimum of three periods or the equivalent, while students at the intermediate levels of proficiency receive a minimum of two periods or the equivalent, and more advanced students receive a minimum of one period a day (REL-NEI, 2013). Pennsylvania has published guidelines to consider when planning daily direct instruction for English language learners (PDE, 2009). They are as follows:

Level 1: Entering
2 hours

Level 2: Beginning
2 hours

Level 3: Developing
1-2 hours

Level 4: Expanding
1 hour

Level 5: Bridging
up to 1 hour (or support dictated by student need)

Figure 2.3 A tool for understanding services offered

Teacher:

Caseload:

1. Number of active (non-monitored) ELLs in your caseload:

2. Number of monitored ELLs in your caseload:

3. Number of schools that you serve:

4. Additional responsibilities that you have:

5. Are you full time or part time (indicate %) status?

Grouping patterns:

6. Indicate how grouping decisions are made. Students are grouped according to:

_____ Their language proficiency levels

_____ The strategies they need

_____ Their grade levels

_____ Other, or a combination of grouping patterns. Please explain:

Types/amount of services:

6. What model program(s) are you (individually) using? If more than one type, indicate percentage of time you are using each.

_____ % Pull-out

_____ % Coteaching

_____ % Sheltered content instruction

Please indicate the amount of time (on average) that you meet with ELLs of specific proficiency levels.

Proficiency levels	Total # of students in your caseload by proficiency level	Number of minutes/hours seen
Starting		Daily or Weekly (circle one)
Emerging		Daily or Weekly (circle one)
Developing		Daily or Weekly (circle one)
Expanding		Daily or Weekly (circle one)
Bridging		Daily or Weekly (circle one)
Monitored		Daily or Weekly (circle one)
	Frequency with which records for monitored students are reviewed:	

Indicate any special circumstances that might affect the way the data appear. For example, elaborate on students that are shared between two teachers' caseloads, or where the amount of time might appear skewed for that proficiency level.

Check with your state department regarding the number of recommended hours of ESL/EAL instruction for your ELLs.

Do observe ESL/EAL lessons

You don't need to be a linguist to begin to assess the quality of your program's offerings. As the principal, the only way to know what is being offered, is to observe the instruction that is delivered in and out of the ESL/EAL program. Just as walk-throughs, informal, and formal observations support the quality of instruction in your school as a whole (Kachur, Stout, & Edwards, 2010), they will also support the quality of instruction in your ESL/EAL program while they help you develop your own expertise in ESL/EAL programming.

As you observe ESL/EAL lessons, ask yourself these 3 questions:

1. What do the students need?
2. How is the instruction that I am observing supporting that need?
3. How is the instruction that I am observing

supporting the ELLs' success in the content classroom?

As you observe content lessons, consider sitting beside the ELL(s) for a portion of the lesson. Ask yourself these questions:

Regarding the ELLs

- Why are they excelling or struggling?
- How are they doing?
- With what are they excelling or struggling?
- Why are they excelling or struggling?

Regarding Instruction

- In order to make this lesson accessible to ELLs, what do they need?
- How are the content and readings scaffolded to provide access to complex texts and concepts?

Regarding Interactive Structures

- Where instruction is delivered in English, are ELLs provided opportunities for classroom interactions around the content with their non-ELL peers?

Regarding Evidence of Learning

- What evidence is there that ELLs are learning? Is it possible to leave this lesson without having learned? What could have been done to ensure evidence of learning? (Try using *Total Participation Techniques*).

An important reminder

As you observe, keep in mind that teaching in linguistically diverse classrooms is hard work, and it's much easier to notice what is not working from the vantage point of an observer. Try to keep that perspective in mind as you meet to discuss possible strategies for reaching all learners. Teachers will be more likely to acknowledge the need for scaffolds and changes to their instruction if they feel that their efforts are appreciated, and if they feel as though you acknowledge and are supporting them with the challenges that they are facing.

In a nutshell...

Too many programs are haphazardly assembled because the term ELLs is seen as a blanket label. ELLs are not the same. Prior schooling experiences play a significant factor in determining what students will need. The question, "What do they need?" ought to guide grouping decisions. By asking pointed questions, school leaders can go a long way in ensuring that ESL/EAL programs are actually supporting ELLs in their academic and linguistic development. In this chapter, several tools were provided to ensure program quality.

3

You Shouldn't Always Trust What You Hear

Academic language is essential for success in school. Without it, ELLs will not be able to be successful past the primary grades. Because of the misunderstandings that academic language often causes, grasping the distinction between conversational language and academic language is critically important. While educators may consciously agree that there is a difference between conversational and academic language, in practice, we see that expectations with regard to student performance are often based on teachers' perceptions of students' conversational skills. As Jim Cummins (1984) found, in his seminal research decades ago, this can often lead to a high number of ELL referrals for special education services, when the problem actually stems from a lack of academic language proficiency resulting in a difficulty with tasks that require a high degree of academic language. Consider the following conversations, one with a student who is an ELL and the other with a non-ELL.

Conversation with Marcos, an ELL (Marcos is a long-term English learner)

Marcos	I'm gonna need some time with the book report, 'cuz my uncle died and the funeral is tomorrow.
Teacher	I'm so sorry to hear about your uncle. I understand. How much time will you need?
Marcos	I don't know, like, maybe Friday.
Teacher	Of course, I can do that. So, the book

report will now be due on Friday for you.
Again, I'm so sorry about your uncle. Did
he live in this area?

Conversation with Peter, a non-ELL

Peter   I'm gonna need some time with the book
          report, 'cuz my uncle died and the funeral
          is tomorrow.

Teacher I'm so sorry to hear about your uncle. I
          understand. How much time will you need?

Peter   I don't know, like, maybe make it due
          on Friday.

Teacher Of course, I can do that. So, the book report
          will now be due on Friday for you. Again,
          I'm so sorry about your uncle. Did he live in
          this area?

At this point you're probably wanting to go back
and carefully scan for the differences between the
two conversations. Allow us to save you some time,
and tell you that there weren't any major differences.
Both Marcos and Peter used conversational English
to get their messages across. When it comes to
short functional conversations, Marcos and Peter
sound pretty much the same. Unless we're asking
open-ended questions that we are going to be
intentionally analyzing for certain linguistic features,
it's often difficult to tell the difference between

our ELLs who are conversational and our non-ELLs. Therein lies the problem, which often leads educators to believe that because Marcos and Peter sound the same, their performances should also be the same. When tasks that require academic reading and writing lead to drastically different outcomes, educators are often left to wonder if cognitive disabilities are to blame, when actually the answer lies in the ELL's ability to comprehend, read, and write using academic English.

Conversational language is acquired relatively quickly for English language learners. Students are often conversational within a year or two after arriving in English speaking schools. Academic language, on the other hand, consists of vocabulary and linguistic complexities that can take years to acquire. Researchers estimate that it takes about 5-7 years to acquire academic language (Cummins, 1991; Hakuta, Butler, & Witt, 2000). That estimate jumps to 7-10 years for students who are not literate in their home language (Thomas & Collier, 1997, 2002). More current data supports these estimates in that it would take approximately eight years to exit, or reclassify, the current pool of English language learners receiving ESL/EAL services (see Himmele, Himmele, & Potter, 2014).

The misunderstandings between conversational and academic language proficiencies can have substantially negative impacts on how teachers approach teaching and learning for students who haven't acquired the academic proficiencies that their non-ELL peers have acquired. As noted earlier, the biggest problems may arise from the fact that the ELL and the non-ELL peers often sound similar in informal classroom conversations, confirming to the teacher that ELLs should be performing at about the same levels without scaffolded instruction and needed supports. When teachers, who may have carried on a comprehensible conversation with a child just minutes ago, believe that students are more linguistically proficient than they actually are, much needed support goes lacking.

The impact of academic language

There is an activity that has appeared in our books,

and that we often do in our presentations. We'd like to present it here, because it does a quicker, more effective job of expressing the importance of academic language than if we were to drone on for 40 more pages. The paragraph we've selected is from an older fifth grade history book. We call it *The Blah Activity*, and we encourage you to use it with your teachers during a faculty meeting or during a professional development session. (Appropriate citations would be appreciated.)

The "Blah" Activity

First, read the paragraphs and underline every word that would not be considered conversational English for a typical fifth grader. In other words, if you wouldn't hear the word used on the playground by a typical fifth grader, then underline it. (Note: Please ignore any content-specific history words, since those would typically be taught by the teacher. For this activity, we'd like to focus on non-content specific academic words.)

Grant seemed an ideal leader to unite the nation. Bearded, muscular, and overly fond of cigars, he was admired as the Civil War general who had faced down Confederate General Robert E. Lee. He was also known for his generous terms of surrender to the Confederate armies.

A gentle, modest man, Grant brought a quiet dignity to the White House. During the Civil War, he had disliked the fancy trappings of high military rank. As President, he refused to take advantage of his position. When he received a $20 speeding ticket for driving his carriage too fast, he paid it.

Yet Grant was not able to impose his standards on other members of the Republican Party. Despite his promise of peace, Grant's presidency was plagued by political conflicts, corruption, and scandal. (Viola, 1998, p. 646)

Next, divide up into groups of three, with each person assigned one of the three paragraphs.

Ask each participant to read his or her paragraph out loud in the order it appears. Wait! There's a catch: When they read it out loud, they should replace any underlined word with the word "Blah."

After they read it, ask participants to discuss these three prompts:

    1. How does academic language affect

reading for ELLs and students who have only acquired a modest level of academic language?

2. What is an *Aha* that you have regarding ELLs and reading in the content areas, or regarding your experiences with ELLs in your own classroom?

3. What now? How might you support ELLs in being successful with reading in your classroom?

Literacy in the home language

For most students who are not literate in their home language, reading and writing are the most difficult of the four linguistic domains to master. (The four domains are listening, speaking, reading, and writing.) The results of these misunderstandings are often to blame for the historically high over-representation of English language learners in special education programs. A lack of understanding of the differences between academic and conversational language may cause teachers to falsely assume that a student simply lacks motivation or is cognitively incapable of succeeding, when what that student really needs is scaffolded instruction and opportunities to build academic language and content at the same time. The answer is not to remove the obstacles of reading and writing. The answer is to scaffold the reading and writing so that students can not only be successful with the task at hand, but also acquire important skills in reading that will support their academic language growth and their overall academic growth.

The answer is not to remove the obstacles of reading and writing. The answer is to scaffold the reading and writing.

It is estimated that a third of English language learners drop out of school (EPE, 2009). Most of the United States' population of ELLs speak Spanish as a home language. For Latinos, as a whole, drop-out rates may actually be closer to 48% (EPE, 2008). Thomas and Collier found that, with regard to programming, the largest numbers of dropouts came from those ELLs whose parents refused language support services. Additionally, the worst performance for ELLs was seen for those students whose programs were limited to three years or less. Conversely, the best performance was seen for ELLs who benefitted from bilingual programming (Thomas & Collier, 2002). Keep that in mind, because the student's home language is your best ally, and as described in Figure 2.1, the stronger the student's academic language proficiency in his or her home language, the better his or her academic performance in English.

A student who is acquiring academic language in the home language will easily transfer that fancy language, the ability to think critically, and new concepts and knowledge into English. On the other hand, those who have not acquired academic levels of proficiency in the home language must learn complex concepts in a weaker language, without being able to anchor these concepts to what has already been learned. This becomes a much more difficult journey for them than for their ELL peers who have academic proficiency in their home languages. Additionally, parents should continue to speak in the home language to children, not only because it is detrimental and impractical for parents to use a weaker language at home, but also because it helps children to continue to strengthen their proficiency in their home language, which ultimately ends up helping their growth in English.

Every teacher

Next, it's important to analyze the level and complexity of support that we offer English language learners. We don't lose English language learners, when they arrive as non-English speakers. At the point when it is obvious that they need linguistic supports, teachers are empathetic and understanding that a student with a thick accent, newly arrived, needs their support. However, that empathy and support is likely to be diminished for a student who sounds like his or her non-ELL peers, but who still desperately needs the support of scaffolded reading and writing experiences. We don't lose ELLs when they first arrive. We lose them when they can already speak English. We don't see the worst performance for English language learners when they are directly receiving ESL/EAL services; we see their worst performance once they've learned enough English to no longer qualify for ESL/EAL services.

By that time, many English language learners sound similar to their non-ELL peers, and the achievement gap not only persists, but it widens (Thomas & Collier, 2002).

We don't lose ELLs when they first arrive. We lose them when they can already speak English.

The implications of this are clear, if we are going to support our ELLs, we will not only need to address the services that they receive in ESL/EAL, but we will especially need to address the type of learning opportunities that exist in their non-ESL/EAL classrooms—their content classrooms. Again, we will need to support all teachers in helping ELLs succeed, not just the ESL/EAL teachers.

More than a year's growth

The average English language learner (ELL) makes 6-8 months of growth for every 10 months of growth made by their typical non-ELL peers (Thomas & Collier, 1997, 2002). A loss of 20% to 40% of academic growth for just one year may be addressed through standard teaching practices, but a persistent 20% to 40% loss that is accumulated annually requires excellence in teaching, and requires the type of educators that are determined to make the most of every teaching opportunity in order to accelerate learning as well as academic language growth. In order to bridge the persistent achievement gap between ELLs and non-ELL peers, ELLs will need to make more than a year's growth every year. That means that every teacher needs to be invested in supporting academic language growth and achievement, not just ESL/EAL teachers.

In a nutshell...

A whopping 65% of ELLs were born in the continental United States (Swanson, 2009). By far, the majority of ELLs are conversational, and those that are not, will soon be conversational. The first picture that teachers often get of an ELL is that of a brand new arrival. Strategies for new arrivals are important, for example, using visuals and labeling a classroom. However, too many ELLs fly under the radar of teachers' attention, because they seem to speak English fluently. There is a huge difference between the language that is spoken by students, and the type of language that is found in books, and that is required to understand academic texts. Conversational language and academic language are different. It can take 5–10 years for a student who is conversational to acquire the academic linguistic proficiency that is comparable to that of non-ELL peers. All teachers need to know this, because it alerts them to the need for instructional scaffolds that will help them to frame lessons that build academic language and content at the same time.

There Are Ways to Support ELLs in Developing Academic Language. The CHATS Framework Can Help

Teachers' apprehensions are high when it comes to teaching ELLs. In fact, a recent survey showed that teachers' concerns over teaching the Common Core State Standards were greatest when it came to making these standards accessible to English language learners (EPE, 2013). It's what worried them the most, even more than teaching the Common Core to students with special needs.

Teachers' concerns over teaching the Common Core State Standards were greatest when it came to making these standards accessible to ELLs.

We won't pretend that teaching English language learners is not hard work. It is. There is no well-designed pre-packaged curriculum that can support academic language development and growth in the content areas. Though it may seem like an easy solution, investing in actual ESL curricula is often a poor use of funds and resources because of the vast complexities inherent in learning a language. So much of learning a language is dependent upon a student's prior history in his or her home language(s), home environments, outside experiences, and current abilities in literacy. Teaching ELLs well takes teacher expertise and consistent uses of formative assessments. Because of that, teachers will need to be adept at creating engaging classrooms that intentionally teach content while at the same time immersing students in experiences that grow academic language.

The CHATS Framework

It is important that every teacher understand ways to support students in their content learning as well as their academic language development. There are several ways that conversational students' academic progress can be accelerated. We'll briefly present these in five general points that support classroom environments where language and content are learned together. To make these easier to remember, these are presented using the acronym found in our CHATS Framework. The CHATS acronym stands for the following:

C Content reading supports

H Higher-order thinking opportunities

A Assessment (frequent checks for understanding)

T Total participation techniques

S Scaffolds (using technology and imagery to support complex readings)

CHATS is the topic of our 2009 ASCD book, *The Language-Rich Classroom: A research-based framework for teaching English language learners.* We'll provide a very brief overview here, but you can also refer to the book if you would like more thorough research-based explanations and specific examples of how to embed teaching techniques that support teachers in each of the five components of the framework.

Content reading supports

For students who are not literate in their home language, as well as for many who are, reading and writing are typically the most difficult of the language domains to master. The classroom will need to be a place where students are drawn to great books and drawn to the content. Reading and writing experiences will need to be scaffolded to allow for student comprehension, engagement, and deeper reading. Teachers will have to work a little harder to help students make personal connections that build student interest and that prepare the students to delve into the readings. Comprehension strategies will need to be emphasized at all grade levels. (For simple tools for supporting comprehension, accuracy, fluency and vocabulary growth in the primary grades, see Boushey & Moser, 2009.)

Academic language is found in books

Read-alouds are essential, because they provide an immersive experience in the language of text. Academic language can be found in literature as well as in informational texts (Himmele & Himmele, 2012, 2014). Read-alouds not only provide exposure to sophisticated language, they also provide exposure to the on-grade level and above grade level language that students are oftentimes not capable of reading yet, but are fully capable of comprehending. This is the non-content specific type of language typically found in students' content reading books. Audiobooks are a great tool, too, and ought to be especially encouraged as an in-school and out-of-school tool for building academic language, especially when accompanied by a hard copy text with which students can use to read along.

At the elementary grades, consider implementing a reading structure that maximizes the amount of time that students spend actually reading, as opposed to learning about reading. *The Daily 5* (Boushey & Moser, 2014) is one such plan that can help teachers to structure their schedules in a way that prioritizes time spent reading, while also helping them to differentiate and target specific strategies that students need. The reality is that struggling readers spend far too little time in high-success reading. Gambrell, Wilson, and Gantt (2001) found that poor readers spent more time learning about how to read, and practicing isolated sounds outside of the context of good books, while good readers spent more time actually reading.

According to Richard Allington, "The experimental evidence is clearer today than a decade ago, that the actual volume of reading activity is an important component in the development of a myriad of reading proficiencies." Still, rather than provide poor readers with access to high success reading opportunities, "we fill struggling readers' days with tasks that require little reading" (Allington, 2013, p.526). We have found this to be disappointingly true when observing reading lessons with ELLs. Even when students are proficient enough to experience success in reading, they spend much of their time learning *about* reading. It's a simple formula, if ELLs are to become proficient readers, they will need to spend a lot of time in high success reading.

Metacognitive skills are also critical, because the students have to be just as proactive about their learning as their teachers are, and just as intentional about building their own academic language as are their teachers. Remember, that in order to bridge the achievement gap, students will need to make more than a year's worth of growth every year.

Writing is hard

For most of the ELLs whom we've interviewed, particularly for the long-term English learners who lack strong literacy skills in their home languages, writing is by far the most onerous of the four language domains (listening, speaking, reading and writing). When it comes to writing, frequent and relevant mini-lessons are essential. Making use of mentor texts is an excellent way to teach writing (Dorfman & Cappelli, 2007). This is particularly true because so many ELLs lag behind in reading, thus they haven't experienced good writing examples from dearly loved books. Writing is hard. It will need to be heavily scaffolded, first through discussion or other ways of getting students to flesh out their thoughts. The best writing comes from inspiration. In other words, the best writing comes from people who really have something to say. So, teachers have to get students to the point where they really have something to say. The writing process and writing workshops are essential components of quality writing experiences that support English language learners (Fletcher & Portalupi, 2001; Lane, 2016). Writing frameworks can help, but don't neglect the more authentic writing experiences, such as the use of everyday simple writer's notebooks (Fletcher, 1996).

Implicit/explicit academic language development

Academic language needs to be taught implicitly as well as explicitly. One of our favorite quotes is by a researcher named Stephen Krashen. In his words, "language is too vast, too complex, to be taught or learned one rule or word at a time" (2006). In order to help students develop the academic language that they'll need, it will take a combination of implicit and explicit approaches toward language development. We like to remind teachers of four keys to developing academic language.

Four keys for developing academic language:

1. Speak it.
2. Read it.
3. ZPD it.
4. Teach it.

Implicit approaches of vocabulary development refer to the creation of a language-rich classroom, where teachers *speak it* (they frequently use the academic language in ways that are comprehensible to students), *read it* (they immerse students in meaningful reading and read-aloud experiences), and *ZPD it* (*ZPD it* refers to using Vygotsky's zone of proximal development and the interactive structures of *Total Participation Techniques*, where students are immersed in meaningful classroom interactions that use and rely on content-based interactive discussions). *Teach it* refers to explicit language approaches involving the direct teaching of academic vocabulary and the way it is used in text. Just as it is important to create language-rich classrooms where students soak in academic language-rich experiences, it is also important to teach academic vocabulary and language directly. This is particularly true when readings consist of specific vocabulary that is key to students' reading comprehension.

Higher-order thinking

For all students, you want the content to matter. The content is more likely to matter and to be remembered when students are required to really think about what they are learning. Opportunities for developing higher-order thinking as it pertains to the content will not only cause the learning to be more lasting, it will also be more engaging for your ELLs, as well as your non-ELLs.

We know that for too many ELLs, the cognitive intensity of lessons is diminished when compared to those offered to non-ELL peers. ELLs are not given the same access to higher-order learning opportunities, and they are often relegated to lessons that focus on basic skills to the exclusion of developing critical thinking skills (Verplaetse, 1998; Gándara, 2015). This problem persists, even after ELLs have attained a higher level of conversational proficiency. The result is that ELLs not only struggle with a persistent achievement gap, but they also struggle with what Chambers referred to as the receivement gap (2009). In other words, they aren't even exposed to the opportunities for deeper learning that are presented to their non-ELL peers.

ELLs are not given the same access to higher-order learning opportunities, and they are often relegated to lessons that focus on basic skills to the exclusion of developing critical thinking skills.

Rippling

There are simple teaching techniques for promoting

opportunities for deeper learning and reflection, which we discuss in our books (2009, 2011), but probably the simplest way of doing this is to adopt a technique that we refer to as rippling (2011). Rippling is the opposite of the traditional Q & A that characterizes many classrooms today. It starts with a higher-order prompt that is posed to every learner. Within that first step is an opportunity for all students to respond to the prompt. For example, this may be done in the form of a Quick-Write, where all students jot down their thoughts on paper. In the second step, students share their individual responses with pairs or small groups. The third step involves the teacher then posing the prompt to the class, allowing volunteers to share their responses, or using an interactive structure that allows all students to share their responses. We call this a ripple, because the first step represents the initial plunk of a pebble in a pond; all students individually respond to the prompt. The second step is represented by the resulting ripple; students share in pairs or small groups. This is followed by the third step, the outer ripple, where the prompt is shared with the whole class (see **Figure 4.1**). When compared to the traditional Q & A, the ripple provides opportunities and expectations that all students respond to higher-order prompts.

Assessments (frequent checks for understanding)

When it comes to English language learners, the end of a lesson or unit is often too late to correct misunderstandings. For obvious reasons, frequent checks for understanding need to be an essential part of every lesson. It is also critical that all students, and ELLs in particular, provide teachers with evidence of learning. If something is important enough to teach, then teachers ought to gather evidence that all of their students learned it. Total Participation Techniques can help in this area.

In addition to checking for understanding with regard to the content, understanding where the students are linguistically is also important. Proficiency assessments need to be in the hands

Figure 4.1   Ripple questioning

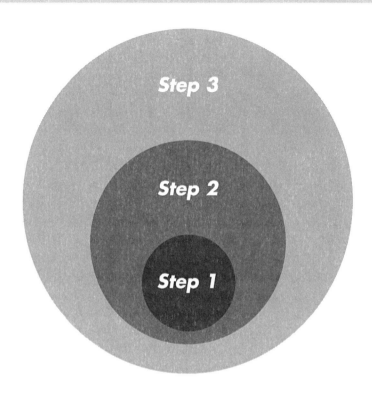

Step 1
All students respond individually to a higher-order prompt

Step 2
Students share responses in pairs or small groups

Step 3
Volunteers or selected students share with the whole class

of the classroom teacher, not just the ESL teacher. For additional resources and information regarding how to go about doing this, see our 2009 book, *The Language-Rich Classroom*, which includes language assessment tools that any classroom teacher can use with their ELL. They require no special training and no knowledge of the ELLs' home languages.

Total Participation Techniques

Teachers should be prepared to use cognitively engaging activities that demonstrate active participation by all the students at the same time. These should rely on the use of questions and prompts that allow students opportunities to develop higher-order thinking. We call these techniques Total Participation Techniques (Himmele & Himmele, 2011). Total Participation Techniques (TPTs) are teaching techniques that provide teachers with evidence of active participation and cognitive engagement from all students at the same time. A study conducted with 211 fifth grade English language learners in four North Texas schools (two were TPT-practicing schools and two were non-TPT practicing schools) concluded that ELLs in the TPT schools performed better on the state's standardized reading assessment than ELLs in the non-TPT schools. Of the monitored ELLs who had been exited from ESL/EAL programs within two years of when the study was conducted, those in the TPT schools outperformed those in the non-TPT schools on standardized reading assessments (de la Isla, 2015). TPTs are important for all students, but they are essential for students learning English as an additional language.

It is very important that we realize that students do not learn language in a vacuum. The best linguistic models for English language learners are their more proficient peers, which is why it is imperative that we create classrooms where students interact with each other about the content being learned. In other words, in a linguistically diverse classroom, passive learning is never an option. Students need to be cognitively engaged, providing teachers with evidence of learning during every lesson that is taught, and classroom interactions need to be intentionally structured around the content.

It is very difficult to maintain attention and focus in a language in which you are weak, which makes unscaffolded lectures deadly to English language learners. Teachers of linguistically diverse classrooms can't just assume that when students are maintaining eye contact, they are following along or understanding. Teachers need evidence, before students leave, that every lesson results in student learning. As noted earlier, English language learners, make an average of six to eight months growth for every ten months of academic growth made by their non-ELL peers. They do not have quality learning time to spare. We cannot afford to make wrong assumptions. Every single lesson needs to result in evidence of student learning.

As you observe lessons, ask yourself these three questions:

1. If I were a student, would I be required to learn at several points during this lesson?
2. If I were a student, would the teacher know when I was not learning?
3. If I were a student, do the prompts ensure

that I would be provided opportunities to develop higher-order thinking?

If any of the answers to these questions are "No," and cause concern with regard to the typical student, then they should cause even greater concern for your ELLs.

Scaffolding

In order to help ELLs read complex texts, you'll need to help prepare them by building background knowledge. Using non-linguistically dependent tools can go a long way in developing enough of an interest so that students are prepared to understand the readings. Things like the use of well-selected technology, word sorts, visuals, pictures, and short videos can help provide enough introductory information to make what was once an insurmountable task doable. You may be wondering what the impact of this scaffolded instruction will be on your non-ELL population. The best thing about scaffolds is that all students benefit from them.

In a nutshell...

Instruction that builds language and content at the same time is characterized by the following:

C Content reading supports

H Higher-order thinking opportunities

A Assessment and frequent checks for understanding

T Total participation techniques (evidence of participation and cognitive engagement)

S Scaffolded reading and writing experiences through the use of non-linguistic tools

Classroom interactions should be specifically planned around content-based discussions that also provide teachers with evidence of learning from all students at several points during every lesson.

We kept this text short and sweet, but here's where to find more...

Conclusion

We want to thank you for making it to the end of this book! We can't emphasize enough how important your role is for ensuring outstanding programs that help ELLs in bridging a persistent achievement gap. To revisit our four things that every principal should know, here they are again in the order that they appear in this book:

1. The quality of your program is highly dependent upon your expertise.
2. ELLs are not all the same, so it matters how you group them.
3. You shouldn't always trust what you hear.
4. There are ways to support your ELLs in developing academic language. The CHATS Framework can help.

We hope that you've come away feeling empowered with big ideas as well as practical tools for supporting the growth of your English language learners. Our goal was to provide you with an overall view of your role as a school leader in supporting your English language learners. We wanted to keep it short and practical. However, there are tools that provide more extensive coverage of how to support your English language learners.

The U. S. Department of Education provides a free

resource, *English Learner Toolkit*, which is available for download (OELA, 2015). It was compiled by the National Center for English Language Acquisition. The toolkit is available by doing a Google search with the key words: "OELA English learner toolkit" or by visiting the link listed in the references of this text. This document has hundreds of links that will provide you with articles and practical tools related to compliance and maintaining a high-quality program.

If you'd like actual strategies for supporting ELLs using the CHATS framework for planning, see our 2009 ASCD book, *The Language-Rich Classroom: A research-based framework for teaching English language learners*. If you'd like examples of teacher-tested techniques that provide evidence of active participation and cognitive engagement, see our 2011 book, *Total Participation Techniques: Making every student an active learner*. There is also an accompanying *Total Participation Techniques* DVD available through ASCD. Free CHATS, TPT, and professional development resources are available on our website *www. TotalParticipationTechniques.com*. The teaching tools in these resources will support all of your students, but are especially essential for your English language learners.

Subscribing to EdWeek's *Learning the Language* blog can help to keep you up to date on the latest policy issues as they relate to schooling for English language learners. Valuable links to research and resources are often provided, and you can subscribe to an RSS feed that will deliver the blog directly to your email inbox. You can find it by doing a Google search for "EdWeek Learning the Language."

For school leaders that are looking to create a school-wide approach toward supporting ELLs' growth, we encourage you to consider reviewing *Four Things Every Teacher Should Know About English Language Learners*. It is the companion text to this text, and is written with classroom and content area teachers as the main audience. The chapters are aligned to the chapters in this text, and while some of the content is repeated, it is written with the goal of helping classroom and content area teachers shape instruction in ways that support

ELLs in their linguistic and academic growth. The chapters are as follows:

1. ***Chapter 1*** Your expertise and ability to provide linguistic and academic scaffolds are vital.
2. ***Chapter 2*** ELLs are not all the same, thus they'll need different things.
3. ***Chapter 3*** You shouldn't always trust what you hear.
4. ***Chapter 4*** There are ways to support your ELLs in developing academic language. The CHATS Framework can help.

Again, on behalf of your English language learners, thank you for taking this very important step in the journey toward improved outcomes for your ELLs. We'd love for you to keep in touch by emailing us and letting us know where the journey takes you. We can be reached at *languagerich@gmail.com*.

References

Allington, R. L. (2013). What really matters when working with struggling readers. *The Reading Teacher*, 66(7), 520-530.

Boushey, G., & Moser, J. (2009). *The CAFE Book: Engaging all students in daily literacy assessment and instruction*. Portland, MN: Stenhouse.

Boushey, G., & Moser, J. (2014). *The Daily 5: Fostering literacy independence in the elementary grades*. Portland, MN: Stenhouse.

Chambers, T. V. (2009). The "receivement gap": School tracking policies and the fallacy of "the achievement gap." *Journal of Negro Education*, 78(4), 417-431.

Cummins, J. (1984). *Bilingual Education and Special Education: Issues in assessment and pedagogy*. San Diego: College Hill.

Cummins, J. (1991). The role of primary language development in promoting educational success for language minority students. In *Schooling and language minority students: A theoretical framework*. CA Office of Bilingual Education (Ed.). (pp. 51-82). Los Angeles: Evaluation, Dissemination and Assessment Center, California State University.

De la Isla, A. (2015). Total participation techniques to increase academic language in English language learners. Unpublished doctoral dissertation, Dallas Baptist University, Dallas, TX.

Dorfman, L. R., & Cappelli, R. (2007). Mentor texts: *Teaching writing through children's literature, K-6*. Portland, Me: Stenhouse Publishers.

EPE (2008). *Diplomas Count*. Bethesda, MD: Educational Projects in Education, Inc.

EPE (2009). *Perspectives on a population: English-language learners in American Schools*. Bethesda, MD: Educational Projects in Education, Inc.

EPE (2013). *Findings from a national survey of teacher perspectives on the Common Core*. Bethesda, MD: Educational Projects in Education Research Center.

Fletcher, R. J. (1996). *A writer's notebook: Unlocking the writer within you*. New York: Avon Books.

Fletcher, R. J. (2001). *Writing workshop: The essential guide*. Portsmouth, NH: Heinemann

Freeman, D. E., & Freeman, Y. S. (with S. Mercuri) (2002). *Closing the achievement gap: How to reach limited-formal-schooling and long term English learners*. Portsmouth, NH: Heinemann.

Gambrell, L. B.., Wilson, R. M., & Gantt, W. N. (2001). Classroom observations of task-attending behaviors of good and poor readers. *Journal of Educational Research*, 74(6), 400-404.

Gándara, P. (2015). *The implications of deeper learning for adolescent immigrants and English language learners*. Students at the Center: Deeper Learning Research Series. Boston, MA: Jobs for the Future.

Hakuta, K., Butler, Y. G., & Witt, D. (2000). *How long does it take English learners to attain proficiency?* University of California Linguistic Minority Research Institute Policy Report 2000-1. Stanford University.

Himmele, P., & Himmele, W. (2009). *The language-rich classroom: A research-based framework for teaching English language learners.* Alexandria, VA: ASCD

Himmele, P., & Himmele, W. (2011). *Total participation techniques: Making every student an active learner.* Alexandria, VA: ASCD

Himmele, P., & Himmele, W. (2012, December 6). Why read alouds matter more in the age of the Common Core. *ASCD Express*, 8(5). http://www.ascd.org/ascd-express/vol8/805-himmele.aspx

Himmele, P., & Himmele, W. (with K. Potter) (2014). *Total literacy techniques: Tools to help students analyze literature and informational texts.* Alexandria, VA: ASCD

Lane, B. (2016). *After the end: Teaching and learning creative revision.* 2nd ed. Portsmouth, NH: Heinemann.

Kachur, D. S., Stout, J. A., & Edwards, C. L. (2010). *Classroom walkthroughs to improve teaching and learning.* Larchmont, NY: Eye on Education.

Krashen, S. D. (1985). *The Input Hypothesis; Issues and implications.* Torrance, CA: Laredo Publishing Company, Inc.

Krashen, S. D. (2004). *The power of reading: Insights from the research.* Portsmouth, NH: Heinemann/ Libraries Unlimited.

OELA (2015). *English learner toolkit for state and local education agencies (SEAs and LEAs)* http://www2.ed.gov/about/

offices/list/oela/english-learner-toolkit/index.html

PDE (2009) *Educating Students with Limited English Proficiency (LEP) and English Language Learners (ELL)* 22 Pa. Code §4.26 DATE OF ISSUE: July 1, 2001 DATE OF REVIEW: April 14, 2009 http://www.education.pa.gov

REL-NEI (2013). *Document reviewing the state regulations of instructional time requirements for English language learners, prepared for Regional Educational Laboratory at EDC* (Northeast & Islands). Available at: file:///C:/Users/phimmele/Desktop/RELNEI_RD0135_Instructional_Time_English_Proficiency.pdf

TESOL. (2006). *TESOL Pre-K-12 English Language Proficiency Standards Framework*. Available at: http://www.tesol.org/advance-the-field/standards/prek-12-english-language-proficiency-standards

Thomas, W. P., & Collier, V. P. (1997). *School effectiveness for language minority students*. Washington, DC: National Clearinghouse for Bilingual Education.

Thomas, W. P., & Collier, V. P. (2002). *A national study of school effectiveness for language minority students' long-term academic achievement.* Washington, DC: Office of Educational Research and Improvement.

Swanson, C. B. (2009). *Perspectives on a population: English-language Leaners in American Schools.* Bethesda, MD: Educational Projects in Education Research Center.

Viola, H. J. (1998) *Why we remember: United States history*. Menlo Park, CA.: Addison Wesley.

Verplaetse, L. S. (1998, Autumn). *How content teachers interact with English language learners*. TESOL Journal, pp. 24-28.

About the authors

Drs. Pérsida and William (Bill) Himmele are Associate Professors in the Early, Middle and Exceptional Education Program at Millersville University in Pennsylvania. Pérsida is a former elementary and middle school teacher and a former district ESL administrator. Bill is a former speech and ESL teacher and higher education administrator. Both are consultants and conduct presentations nationally and internationally. They have two lovely children and a three-legged rescue dog named BoBo. Bill is a die-hard Buffalo Bills and Buffalo Sabres fan (email condolences are always welcomed), and he and his children are PADI certified open-water scuba divers. Pérsida refuses to get her hair wet, which prevents her from obtaining PADI certification, but she loves keeping track of sea turtle nesting and rescue efforts, and experiencing the amazement of watching new hatchlings emerge.

Bill and Pérsida are the authors of several books, including the ASCD bestseller *Total Participation Techniques: Making every student an active learner*. Their website, *www.totalparticipationtechniques.com* contains resources that you may find useful in planning ideal learning environments for ELLs as well as non-ELLs. They welcome your feedback and questions, and can be reached at *languagerich@gmail.com*.

Books by Pérsida and William Himmele include:

Four Things Every Principal Should Know About ELLs: An easy-read for busy educators
Language & Cognition Resources, 2016. By P. Himmele & W. Himmele

Four Things Every Teacher Should Know About ELLs: An easy-read for busy educators
Language & Cognition Resources, 2016. By P. Himmele & W. Himmele

Total Literacy Techniques: Tools to help students analyze literature and informational texts
ASCD, 2014. By P. Himmele & W. Himmele, with K. Potter

Total Participation Techniques: Making every student an active learner
ASCD, 2011. By P. Himmele & W. Himmele
DVD: Total Participation Techniques
ASCD, 2014. By P. Himmele & W. Himmele

The Language-Rich Classroom: A research-based framework for teaching English language learners
ASCD, 2009. By P. Himmele & W. Himmele